Pro Self-developer's search technology,

Site utilization

Professional Self-Developer's Search Technology, Site Utilization

Issued May 25, 2022
Author Moon Sun-Hee
Email perfume007@naver.com

ISBN | 9798831802276

prolog

The role of the U.S. CIA is not to be good at fighting, but to obtain, analyze, and utilize information. Information has various faces. It can be money, save and kill people, bring opportunities, and act as a lubricant to achieve the desired purpose. Information is not necessarily high-dimensional, and does not mean only objectified. The face is as diverse and vast as the stars of the universe, including an individual's tacit knowledge, facts that have not yet been discovered, and information that already exists but has never been utilized.

Everyone knows the importance of big data and data utilization. However, knowing the importance of information and knowing how to use information are different words, and the ability to use information varies widely from person to person. Even if there is information that needs to be checked right now, if you don't have a sense of where the information is, it's easy to search for simple information or waste time wandering around the site. The information found in portal searches is mainly useful for fragmentary things, and the information that is money and valuable is hidden one step further.

Information also has a map. But this information map should be made by individuals, not by selling what someone has made uniform. Even if an information map for a specific field is sold, it is not 100% consistent according to individual needs. And since the quality of information is improved and updated every moment, it is highly likely to achieve the purpose of the search by using the warmest information at this time, not the information map created by someone.

In other words, even if you try to extract the necessary knowledge, you must have a sense of where and what information is, and you must continue to accumulate know-how to use it. This book opens the door. In particular, it focused on institutional sites where information such as treasure, which is easy for people to overlook, is provided free of charge.

The source of information that comes from the distinction between real and fake information, and you don't have to worry about the reliability of the data, is a site run by a public or private company. In addition, even if it is not necessarily an industrial spy or an overseas business trip, related information is disclosed on each overseas institution site. If you want, you can search for information on institutional sites around the world. Non-English speaking countries can use foreign languages as an opportunity to study. However, most reliable sites support English translation.)

With this book as a hint, I hope to become a world powerhouse in the data field that Korea is promoting as a national task in using information knowledge as well as personal success by acquiring and utilizing information that makes money on all institutional sites and making dreams come true.

Turn

Chapter 1 Reasons for Site Utilization

Reasons for Search

It saves time and reduces costs.

It's all my taxes.

You make money when you visit the site.

The benefits of the government and businesses are all application system

Chapter 2 Definition of Site Utilization

Information Retrieval VS Information Exploration

How to look out of the well

Surfing a site

People who are good at searching have a license to search

Chapter 3 Methods of Site Utilization

Exploring information itself is fun

elimination of miscellaneous thoughts

A job search site

The person you want

Chapter V, Act 2 of Punishment

Free career examination and virtual reality job environment experience to explore the second life career path

They're at different levels. They're different

A contest for members to pay allowances

Country   Worker   Recruitment

Information Site

A site where you can find out about government-funded projects for SMEs

Chapter 6 Application for Work

a site that lightens up the company's work

Maintain image quality and reduce capacity

A site that helps college students, office workers, and professional self-developers

Chapter 7 Use for Real Estate Investment

Land Use Planning and Urban Planning Information Site

a real estate investment information site

Chapter 8 Utilizing Local Government Sites

Why local government sites?

Each local government has its own characteristics.

If you visit the site in Gyeonggi-do, you can get a garden for free.

The treasure trove of excellent research materials is also helpful to me economically

The information on local government sites is actually happening.

I can suggest excellent examples of other local governments to the local governments where I live.
local government services

If you look at the contents of the complaint, you can see the opportunity.

Utilization of linkage information between local governments, universities, hospitals, etc

Chapter 9 Utilizing Indirect Political Participation

A practical way to participate indirectly in politics

If you look at the government 24 site, you can see the real power.

Site examples of the Ministry of Public Administration and Security

Korea's Data Warehouse

Creating a Site

Overseas site

Chapter 1 Reasons for Site Utilization

Reasons for Search

《Searching is also a skill that needs to be learned.》

When do we search? When you wake up in the morning to brush your teeth, you search for toothpaste that is good for your gums to shop, prepare for work, and search for the music playlist you want to listen to today. Search for spelling mistakes while writing documents in the office, and search for lunch restaurants. During a conversation with a colleague during lunch time, search for issues that only I don't know and quickly participate in the conversation.

In the afternoon, the Ministry of Education receives a lecture request and searches for related trends to explore related materials.

I decide to become an expert to make my career in the company I work for my own, and search for related certificates and books.

Now, let's think about whether there's a day you didn'

Also, the better you search online, the better you can search and answer. Accuracy is higher, and you can find the information you want faster and more completely. Some people waste half an hour of work that will take less than two minutes to find the desired result.

. The fourth R that students as well as adults should learn in the three skills (3R, Reading, Writing wRiting, Calculating a Rithmetic) that should be taught in pedagogy is research, or search.(Daniel M. Russell, Header The Power of Online Search)

It saves time and reduces costs.

《Information makes more reasonable consumption and less footwork.》

Suppose your research team is looking for a place to keep the elderly, who are experimental, quiet for a week for the project. If you are already a trained information explorer, you can think of a tourism promotion menu operated by each local local government site and summarize it into a few candidates. This will probably reduce the amount of time it takes to travel around the city and find a quiet city (more than a week), the cost of staying, and transportation.

Like this, information saves my time and money. Practical information for my life is on sites run by real−life institutions that are involved in real people's lives. Direct and available information now. This is because it is the policy and business of the institutions that have come out now.

Also, search makes my life more rational. There is a basic hypothesis of economics, saying, "All producers and consumers know all the information related to it and it is perfectly reasonable." This means that the more information you know, whether you are a producer or a consumer, the more reasonable you can make a choice.(〈Keywords to Change the Future, Search 〉〉 Cho Joong Hyuk〉〉)

It's all my taxes.

《《Let's search the local government site first for areas you want to learn and are interested in.》》

Each local government and other government agencies operate courses such as free education, free cultural experiences, and hobbies for the people. This process is all run with my taxes, so let's enjoy it with confidence. For example, free cultural and experience events are announced on this month's cultural event menu on the Incheon City Hall website. During the process, recruitment of volunteers for natural ecology monitoring of Ganghwa Island is of high quality. Volunteers can take courses such as tidal flat ecosystem survey methodology, pay meals during the process, and go to Ganghwa Island to monitor the ecosystem. The result is another line of your career by holding a 'monitoring report' in the form of an exhibition of photos and reports. If you are a natural ecology major or an interested person, you will find an opportunity to take free and high-quality courses. A variety of unexpected and specific free courses are waiting for you on the local government site. Let's participate actively so that we don't waste our taxes.

You make money when you visit the site.

If you check the beauty salon on the Naver portal and make a reservation, you can get a discount of up to 20% for your first visit.

Chapter 2 Definition of Site Utilization

Information Retrieval （索）） VS Information Exploration （索））

· Information retrieval: finding necessary information according to the purpose

· Information Retrieval: To search for or disclose information that has not been revealed

You've probably searched more than primarily for information. That is, we search for information as needed. Both information search and search are important, but the ability to search or search information varies depending on the degree of technology. If you don't know where or what information is, it will take a lot of time to find the information you need, while people with a sense of the organization or site that handles the information will search for quality information more purposefully.

As such, the ability to search for information varies greatly from person to person, and this is an invisible individual competency that turns into problem-solving, benchmarking, and quick response.

Information search is more active than search, and it is an act that does not require information right now. If speed is important for information search, information search is possible only if you invest your time with interest. At this time, searching for information with a purpose requires a low degree of interest, and without a purpose, searching for interest or newness is an act of taking time separately.

Searching for information that people need is hard to get out of their box. I always search for necessary information in my field, and the contents that my colleagues may know at my workplace are the main ones. Therefore, in order to take a differentiation from others and get out of the well, active information search is necessary in addition to information search.

 · Information Retrieval Benefits

 ① an extension of one's thinking range

 ② expansion of the worldview

 ③ Get creative problem-solving information
 ④ Differentiate information skills in
  my workplace (group)

 ⑤ Creating a path to another field

How to look out of the well

Institutional site information search is a specific and applicable behavior that looks outside the well and is currently applicable. What is inside the well and what does it mean for office workers who seem to have the same day every day, or for mothers who are struggling to leave the house due to childcare? It's where and how subordinate the thought is. This brain sometimes reminds me of memories or people that I don't want to think of on my own. If you are an office worker, you are usually a boss or colleague who has to solve work tasks or stresses you out of stress.

The frog in the well is trapped in the idea. It is a frog in a well that lives with problems that you don't have the will to solve, which you just want to avoid even if you think and think about them every day.

To get out of the well, you have to put a brake on your brain and think about something else. Even if I want to think about something else, I can't think of it unless I have something to think of. Don't feel ashamed or stressed out by the jealous and mean employee of my job, there are many people in the world who are much better than that employee. Don't look at him, but think of a better man outside the well and decide to be like him. Then jealousy disappears. I'm telling you, because if you're determined to be like a man outside an extraordinary well, you'll be many times better off than the jealous staff in the well if you follow half of him.

Institutional site information retrieval does not remind me of only where I belong now. It allows you to have a broader world view, such as other companies, other universities, and other local governments. It makes me think big. Then, even in a well, you stand outside the well and look into it. Think of all those institutions as your job or school. However, now consider that you are choosing this place and staying in person and digging deeply.

Hasn't the concept of work gone away? Don't think you own only the house you live in now. All the beaches on the east coast, south coast, and west coast are yours. Let's think that it's yours that you can go and enjoy. The same goes for mountains, and consider all libraries in the world to be your study. In fact, you can go and enjoy it even if you don't have to pay for electricity and clean up yourself, right? This will broaden your horizons, make you a big thinker, and satisfy you even if you don't own a lot.

Surfing a site

We surf our cell phones whenever we have time, whether it's on the subway or waiting for a signal. Cell phone surfing has the effect of relieving stress, but it is a big time when it accumulates and accumulates. Let's surf the site, not the cell phone. There is a function that allows users to create folders by collecting apps on the mobile phone screen. Let's put a site with a similar personality in a folder as a shortcut app. You can visit two to three sites and look through them during the break. The degree of surfing a site in a mobile phone folder is now up to you. Add at least 1 site surfing to your daily routine. When it becomes a habit and embodied, you will unconsciously meet information that makes money and makes your dreams come true through site surfing, not SNS surfing. That minute of success you surf pays for years of failure.

People who are good at searching

Benchmark the behavior of good searchers, reduce search time, and get accurate results.

· Behavior of people who are good at searching within a site

① Before starting a search, make sure what I'm looking for. A common problem among beginners is to start searching blindly without being clear about what the goal is. For example, does it mean 'from the center of the moon to the center of the earth' or 'from the nearest point of the moon to the nearest point of the earth'?It is to do a clear search like this.

② As a searcher, you should understand how confident you are that what you know, what you don't know, and what you know is accurate. The next extended search depends on what you need to know next.

③ In order to understand the information you search, you need context for related content. People who are really good at searching do more than just look for answers to questions. Study materials that talk about the topic, and keep asking yourself what else to know to know if this information fits into a larger context.

④ Which search term should I enter? The answer is basically to search for something that arouses your curiosity.

⑤ People who are good at searching are partly because they already have a wide knowledge of the world So the better you are at searching, the more the world of your knowledge expands. To a wider world of information.

⑥ A new tab is displayed for the search, and terms and concepts that you do not understand are searched in the search results article.

⑦ With the eyes of a third party, I check my search behavior and search method. It searches while checking if it is not a single information-biased search or if it is out of direction.

⑧ People who are really good at searching make a habit of checking whether sources are reliable, consistent with other sources, and accurate. The resources of sites that never admit errors are carefully and value where they acknowledge them.

· the attitude of people who are good at searching within a site

① Resilience: An important difference between just being good at searching and being good at it is the essential attitude of showing resilience in the face of change. This is a positive attitude, that is, the ability to control disappointment and view failure as useful feedback when things don't go your way.

② Persistence is an attitude that continues to challenge. The best combination is sustainability.

③ curiosity to find out more about a field

④ It has the ability to identify more generalized patterns present in the object. In other words, we think of the whole category. For example, when investigating the eating habits of birds belonging to a particular species, it is helpful to find the habits of a higher classification rather than just the habits of the species.

⑤ They also learn from search mistakes, such as not specific search terms.

⑥ Learn the world constantly. The site is constantly changing as new data comes in and old data disappears.

⑦ I'm concentrating. If you look closer at something, take time and look carefully, you'll find almost everything interesting.(Daniel M. Russell, chapter 18)

Search also has a license.

Eligibility means expertise in a particular field. Specialties are those that show more performance skills than ordinary people can usually do in a certain area, and researchers say that expertise can be acquired through very long-term and systematic training. Search also has a license. It is a certificate given to a search expert, i.e., a person who shows more than the level of search ability that ordinary people can do.

· Internet Information Manager: A professional job that searches for information using the Internet. It refers to a person who has professional information search ability to quickly and effectively find the desired information and the latest information on the Internet.

It is also their role to search Internet sites around the world to find and provide information or data in various fields desired by clients as quickly as possible, and to create more value-added secondary information by reprocessing or floating primary information.

They must learn the overall understanding and usage of the Internet and have basic English reading skills. The person in charge of receiving the Doosan Encyclopedia is the Information and Communication Technology Qualification Test (KAIT), and in order to obtain a higher level of qualification, it can be obtained by taking the first written test such as information search strategy and information resource utilization, and passing the second practical test.

Chapter 3 Methods of Site Utilization

Exploring information itself is fun

Humans originally like the process of acquiring new information. The search for information itself is a pleasant act. When I surf the site, it's fun, but it's not a waste of time because it's actually helpful information to me. It also makes you feel the same way as when you find a new restaurant.

Information search is a trip. The information on the agency's site is so vast that it is a hidden treasure before you visit it yourself. Let's visit the institutional site as if we're traveling. Information operated and provided by institutions is more reliable and valuable than information operated and disclosed by individuals. This is because it is information that involves budget, such as government budgets that are difficult for individuals to operate and operating for corporate profits.

Elimination of miscellaneous thoughts

You must have been annoyed by your boss or complaints when you left work. As soon as I leave the office, worrying doesn't solve it, but I'm the one who gets hurt because of the person's lack of personality. At times like this, let's think of the outside world and get rid of miscellaneous thoughts. It is not easy to think of the outside world that I have never seen or been to.

The agency's site makes me think that this company I'm in isn't everything. You can realize how meaningless it is to be struggling with one person in this company and whether it is like a frog in a well. We have to convince the brain to keep coming up with a bunch of work junk thoughts. When persuading, let my brain actually experience different worlds through the site.

A piece of information

If you try a wine snack called Jamon, I want to try another jamon. So is the information. When you visit an institution site, search and click automatically with the desire to explore information deeper and more diversely. In this process, my information is automatically expanded.

In addition, the discovery of institutional sites is a hint and leads to another world of information. In this process, the area and depth of related knowledge are naturally expanded to become experts.

· How to use the institutional site naturally in everyday life: It is not easy to open a cell phone and search the institutional site directly. Usually, I open a mobile phone app and click on the noticeable posts among the posts posted on the portal or SNS to read them.

Do not stop here, but find the name of the organization mentioned in the post or possibly related to it. Next, if you search the name of the institution again in the search window such as the portal, a link to the site appears in the search result. For example, let's search for a site called the National Assembly's confirmation hearing, not finish reading about the National Assembly hearing in today's article.

As a result, each minister-level candidate currently nominated as a candidate can be seen at a glance on the main screen of the confirmation hearing. In this way, portals or SNS are articles containing the publisher's thoughts in specific information, while institutional sites show all related information without adding or subtracting it.

By clicking on the name of the candidate, all the remarks exchanged at the hearing can be confirmed in writing. It is disclosed without any procedures such as login.

Now, let's make a choice. Will I read some articles as I see them, or will I visit related sites and become an expert by expanding my knowledge?

Articles on the portal are part of the story, and the full information is on the site. You only need to make a habit of finding or recalling relevant site names or organization names in articles or SNS posts. It takes a little effort, of course, to get into this habit.

Let's make it a habit to consciously find the name of the institution, search and look it up. Then you can check the vast amount of quality information on the relevant site whenever you want.

I have never seen a case of continuous use of this tip as a tool even around me. Make sure you use this method that you don't use much. It will bring about competence differentiation in your group.

There are data on institutional and corporate sites that you can't imagine. Let's give it a try. Now.

I want to eat when I know the food.

I didn't know the taste of skate samhap until I tried it. You can think of wanting to eat food only when you know its taste. Likewise, the size of the world in which information is diverse and many people dream is much larger than those who do not.

People who have more information than me live in a bigger world than me. Let's pay attention to how much more diverse and larger a world that person lives in when you look at someone, not in the size of an apartment. The more curious you know, the more you realize that there is a bigger world after that.

At least those who can gauge how big the world can be live a richer life than those who are trapped in my small world and do not even try to expand the world.

Selective focus and navigation

As information search technology is trained, a person who enters a deeper level knows how to do selective intensive search during the information search process.

As you browse the site, you will encounter information on the field of interest or the field you need now. At this stage, a map of related sites is unfolded implicitly in the head.

I can think of several sites that may have details of the information of interest I just met. (Only for those who have visited the site) For this person, all sites in Korea or around the world become their information management room. Not only does the amount of information become vast, but it also becomes an expert in the field.

· Application for regular subscription on the site: Public institutions, large corporations, etc. provide services to apply for subscription to institutional promotional magazines through the website. You can receive it free of charge with paper books, or you can directly view or download it as a PDF on the Internet. You can receive information in the field of interest regularly. Now, go to the website you're interested in, go to the promotional menu, and subscribe to the free agency magazine.

· Example of applying for a regular subscription: If you want to subscribe to a magazine related to the Seoul Metropolitan Government, first open the Seoul Metropolitan Government website. If you look at the top right

of the site, there is usually an icon that you can search in the shape of a magnifying glass. Search for the word subscription. Then, the relevant magazine name is usually searched in the search results. The Seoul Metropolitan Government runs a magazine called Seoul Sarang. This informative magazine is free.
(We receive applications for re-subscription every two years, and the re-subscription fee is also free.)

Very few people know this information. It is very useful information for people who run cafes and restaurants in Seoul. (Because you can have a great Seoul magazine in the store!)

This is just an example, and let's explore whether your site has a regular free subscription service. At the very least, even if it's not a paper magazine, all the newsletter subscriptions will be in operation. Let's sign up for a newsletter with an email address that you always open. You can receive the latest related information every day. (Try searching with various words such as subscription or subscription application or magazine, and know-how to apply for subscription is also accumulated.)

· The site magazine I am interested in applying for subscription: Seoul Love, Jeju Newsletter, etc. are mainly operated by local governments and public institutions for free. Some companies run magazines for a fee, but you can use the free publication of the magazine in PDF files. (For example, the recent 'economic trend' of the Ministry of Strategy and Finance is a paid magazine, but it is released free of charge in PDF files.)

Engraving (Memorizing) Strategies

Differentiation between people with similar information search amounts depends on whether valuable information is engraved and embodied among the searched information.

Depending on the information, there are some information that I have to take out of my brain and use at that moment.

Chapter V, Act 2 of Punishment

Free career examination to explore the second career path, and virtual reality job environment experience

As the average life expectancy increases, there will be more cases of going to college twice. Visit career search sites that are helpful not only for students but also for adults.

I can find a career path that I can enjoy and find information that helps me draw a roadmap according to the career choice. It is good to find a career counselor by investing in transportation and time by selling footwork, but the advantage of visiting the site is that you can search for a career on your phone anytime you want.

· CareerNet: It provides free medical examination. Tests for elementary school students, middle and high school students, college students, and general use can be conducted. In addition, it is full of information on related departments, and the voice of the career field is also provided through interviews with experts in the field through videos.

· Worknet: In addition to job search information, you can experience the job environment in advance with virtual reality, and introduce what you learn in the major that provided career guides for each major at university, major jobs, and job prospects that you can enter after graduation, all of these materials are free.

· Major map: It provides AI-based customized career service, and provides related information clearly based on data analysis when searching for departments, universities, and jobs. For example, when searching for information and communication-related jobs, 39 related jobs are shown. Selecting a data developer provides specific and practical information such as how to have a job, related majors, certificates, wages, job satisfaction, job prospects, job performance, knowledge, work environment, personality, interest, and educational distribution. Don't just choose your career path with vague feelings, but visit this site regularly and prepare for the second half of your life in advance.

They're at different levels. They're different

Government organizations, large corporations, and public institutions provide education for each employee or competency. For example, in the case of the Local Human Resources Development Institute, the admission process is operated for the director-level.

Although it is not possible to enter this admission process, it is possible to check what kind of education they receive. The curriculum allows you to develop yourself with directions, not vague self-development. If you have a promotion goal or position you want, the site is open to all the competencies suitable for the position.

The main contents of the director-level candidate competency curriculum consist of group discussion, oral presentation, role performance, and document box techniques on simulated tasks.

The document-boxing method is to develop managers' decision-making ability, and training participants are provided with information about virtual companies, production products, organizational structure, and members, and then make decisions to solve problems in specific management situations.

In order to select and foster talent in companies, the purpose of evaluating individual performance ability is mainly used. If you're looking to become a director in the future, experiencing a variety of models for discussion, presentation practice, and problem-solving skills should be built up as a major career strategy.

Since it is a competency that has been prepared for a long time when the moment of opportunity comes, the appearance of not being embarrassed and dealing with it clearly has a comparative advantage with the person who has prepared at random.

A contest for members to pay allowances

Local governments and other government agencies must operate committees in accordance with laws and regulations.

In relation to recruiting outside members, public offerings are often posted on the institution's website. You never know this information unless you visit the agency's site.

For example, regarding the mandatory task review committee for software development projects, a local government in Gangwon Province paid allowances (usually around 100,000 won per hour) and announced an article recruiting a pool of task review committee members.

The qualification requirements are as follows, and those with more than six years of work experience in the field of software technology can take the examination only with the department related to the informatization project or proof of work.

The application rate may not be

surprisingly high, so let's tap it. In addition to the allowance, it is also a career where you can put a nice line on your resume. "Appointment of 00:0000 project deliberation committee," your information retrieval ability shines again.

〈Example of qualification requirements for members' competition, competition for members of the software project task review committee〉

▫ Grade 5 or higher officials involved in software work

▫ Assistant Professor and Expert in Software-Related Areas

□ Members or experienced persons of the Intelligent Informatization (Regional Informatization) Committee;

□ 6+ years of experience in software technology

□ Recommender of NIPA (Information and Communication Industry Promotion Agency) and other related agencies and ICT consultative bodies

Country Worker Recruitment Information Site

If you go to the Nara Workplace Recruitment Information Site, you can grasp the necessary capabilities for positions hired in various countries in detail.

Simply, the details of the task and performance are written in detail, not the TOEIC score or any certificate, but what problem-solving skills are needed to perform the task.

If you are preparing for the future and preparing to get a job, let's prepare for the necessary skills sharply and clearly, rather than preparing for the future, and that ability will remain influential even after employment.

A site where you can find out about government-funded projects for SMEs

You can check the announcement of the support project by going to the corporate yard site. For example, the Korea Forest Service can take a general look at projects to support small and medium-sized enterprises such as the announcement of recruitment of participants in this year's forest product global online mall entry support project.

When small and medium-sized companies apply for the project, the companies selected through the evaluation of the selection committee will receive overall support, such as not only supporting actual costs of online marketing but also closely supporting them through matching with professional MDs.

The government also supports small and medium-sized companies that have benefited well because they need some business results.

If you can start with government money, why start a business with my own money.

Since there are various recruitment announcements every time, let's set up a notification and check it from time to time.

Chapter 6 Application for Work

A site that lightens up the company's work

You can't tell the difference from the outside. When you look at how quickly documents are created, the difference in ability is distinguished.

Rather than developing the ability to write documents to be promoted and recognized, let's develop the ability to write documents not to work overtime like a meal under the workload. There is already a lot of information on what to learn on the site below.

Since it is not easy to learn a lot of information in a cramming manner, let's find a need in the process of writing a document and learn the tips one by one.

You can forget about it. You can visit the site again next time and check. If you repeat the process of forgetting and searching a few times like that, the skill becomes mine.

· Smartsheet: You can download various English forms for free. It is a site specializing in project management format. You can benchmark the forms here and make them your own management sheet.(If you always set Papago to be translated into English on your laptop or mobile phone, sites in English will also be automatically translated into Korean and displayed. It is possible to visit not only Korean sites but also sites around the world.)

· Canva: It offers a variety of design templates. There are paid and free versions such as thumbnails, posters, newsletters, announcements, and meeting invitations, and the free version also provides enough designs. By mixing free design, you can create and distribute your own copyright-free design templates, or use them. In fact, there are cases where design templates are created here and sold on the Internet.

· Yesform: It provides a collection of various Korean formats, PPT templates, etc. You can download high-quality PPT and change the contents and use it right away. Let's make PPT as our main task or use it

when   we   have   an   important
announcement.

Maintain image quality and reduce capacity

The site, Tinyping, consists of a simple web screen, which compresses the capacity and maintains image quality as long as the image you want to reduce is good for the square box. Reduce the capacity and use it when you want to maintain the quality.

A site that helps college students, office workers, and professional talent balers

·WVT, ThinkGood: Good for searching for information to participate in contests and external activities.

·If you visit the sites of the thesis-related sites RISS (Academic Information Research Service), KISS (Academic Information Research Service), Google Scholar (Google Academic Search), DBPIA (DBPIA), and the National Assembly Library, you can use various kinds of materials for each site.

·Data survey: Kosis (National Statistical Portal), Gallup Korea

Research Institute (provides various research projects, columns, and reports), Nielsen Korea (statistics related to Internet service trends), National Legal Information Center (refer to the data law), Policy Briefing (general information and welfare). You can usefully find the right materials for you in the welfare center.)) and BigKines (the latest news from 54 major domestic media companies is organized by keywords and provided in the latest trends, so you can quickly search for the information you want.)

·PPT: Two color combination,

SlideSHare (free download and edit PPT slides), Flaction (free download of various icon images, use pictogram images, etc.) and canvas (all designs and edits on site and remove text from background)
·Remember: An app that saves contents on its own when you take a business card

·Mute silence: It is linked to the basic camera to eliminate the camera shutter sound

·X-mind: Free mind map program

·WinMerge: Text File Merger

·UltraViewer: Remote control tool

·VirtualBox: You do not need to install a separate OS by providing a virtual space.

·PhotoScape: Free image editing program

·Background Burner: Transparent image background

·Fixler; Image Editor on the Web

·Pixabay: Site where you can get free high-definition images

·Paperson: Naver Cafe where you can get various document forms

·Free English study site: Use VOA News Special English, but you can study English in which the use of difficult words and complex language structures that make it difficult to read is excluded as much as possible. A native speaker reads the article slowly. NPR (English radio), Project Gutenberg (more than 20,000 won) free download site, USA Learn (three-step support for beginners), English Cube (a lot of English learning materials), Hackers free lectures (free material, etc.), Wacch TV online (free TV streaming) and Heading. Very useful for translation)

·Useful site for graduate school entrance: National graduate school (provided by checking the name of graduate school by region), Dr. Kim (provided information on recruitment of researchers), university notification site (available information on graduate school tuition), 1365 (provided volunteer activity information for preparation of graduate school)

Chapter 7 Use for Real Estate Investment

Land Use Planning and Urban Planning Information Site

I had to visit the district office to check whether the land between the building was made of national land or owned by me. You can go to the land joint site to check the cadastral map, and you can check the area of the address you want to check with the red line.

It clearly shows whether the alley next to the ambiguous house is my land. without any accession procedures or costs In addition, if you are interested in investing in real estate, you can read urban use plans and land use plans officially posted on the site every year.

Wouldn't it increase the probability of success to do it where the government is willing to invest at least when investing?!

A real estate investment information site

·Seoul Metropolitan Government Housing Bureau website: Detailed information on the basic plan for urban residential environment improvement (redevelopment, reconstruction plan, apartment sales information, unsold information, etc.)

· Seoul Metropolitan Government's online public system for handling civil complaints: Search for redevelopment area designations, project implementation authorization, and accurate information as much as the agency's

·Internet land information service: Each province can easily access regional land information, real estate complaint issuance, real estate brokerage information and intellectual land administration information, and obtain information on sales without visiting the site. Useful investment information can also be used on the websites of each city, county, and district offices. In addition to the basic urban plan of local governments, it can be viewed not only through public data such as statistical annual reports, reorganization plans, traffic maintenance plans, and administrative data, but also through public officials in charge.

· Land Corporation, Housing Corporation, and SH Corporation: Providing information on land and housing sales and subscription

· Korea Asset Management Corporation: Information on cheap public offerings, provision of information on sales comparable to court auctions, and detailed search of public notices allows users to search for millions of won worth of land, houses, buildings, and real estate as well as cars, machinery, and real estate

·Supreme Court Internet Registry: Issuance of documents to be checked when obtaining rent or buying a house

·National Federation of Banks: When lending, conditions such as interest rates of banks nationwide can be compared at a glance

· Small business district information

system, National Statistical Office, School Environmental Sanitation Zone, Life Statistics Geographic Service, Korea Appraisal Board Real Estate Statistics, K-BIZ (Small Business District Analysis), Bix-gis (GIS Map Analysis), Industrial Complex Management Corporation (Number of Knowledge Industry Center, occupancy rate, etc.), Nice Biz Map

·Related article information: shopping mall dotcom, sales dotcom, shopping mall 114, maekyung real estate, national and local real estate portal, Join's, shopping mall news radar, CVS Academy (convenience store start-up and commercial district analysis)

·Legal information: Supreme Court (pre-searching, application for judgment), Korea Legal Aid Corporation (legal counseling, legal forms and data), single lawsuit (related to litigation), living law information (living law, real estate law)

Chapter 8 Utilizing Local Government Sites

Why local government sites?

As we pay attention to the work of local governments, there is no one who is not related to local government policies, whether it is private companies or public institutions, small business owners or entrepreneurs. However, the method of throwing away furniture also follows local government standards. Let's teach our children how to use local government information. Let's let them know that my life is closely related to the local government.

Each local government has its own characteristics.

In Korea, eight cities (Seoul, Busan, Daegu, Incheon, Gwangju, Daejeon, Ulsan, Sejong Special Self-Governing City) and nine provinces (Gyeonggi, Gangwon, Chungcheongbuk-do, Chungcheongnam-do, Jeollabuk-do, Jeollanam-do, Gyeongsangbuk-do, and Jeju Special Self-Governing Province) Local government is short for local government. There are also several basic local governments under local governments. Only when you know this can you organically interpret the name of the area with city, county, and ward when looking at the map. Shouldn't I know the name of the country where I live? If you know a lot of food, you can eat a lot, and if you know a lot of local areas, you can leave various possibilities open, whether it's travel or business. If you don't know, you can't dream, you can't try.

If you visit the site in Gyeonggi-do, you can get a garden for free.

Gyeonggi-do Province operates a special service called "Gyeonggi Sharing Service" for Gyeonggi residents.

Any Gyeonggi-do resident can reserve a meeting room, sports activity room, and auditorium operated by Gyeonggi-do and rent it for free, or rent a swimming pool and tennis court as a group to operate the event.

There are also information on various event programs, and there are many free education such as adult volunteer basic education. In addition, a free garden sale service is also in operation so that actual plants can be grown. It's run by the tax of Gyeonggi-do residents, so let's enjoy it proudly. Facilities are well managed and operated by the public, so operation is convenient and more transparent.

·Gyeonggi data analysis portal: Gyeonggi Province provides data on regional economy, statistical information, tourism route recommendation, agriculture, and commercial districts. If a large amount of data analysis is required, it is possible to analyze the raw data of the public and private sectors through an application for use of the Gyeonggi-do Analysis Center.

·A variety of Gyeonggi-do-related sites are operating, including Gyeonggi-do Tourism Portal, Gyeonggi Art Center, Gyeonggi-do Cultural Foundation, Gyeonggi-do Architecture Portal, Design Gyeonggi-do, Gyeonggi Data Dream, and Gyeonggi-do Online Lifelong Learning Knowledge. Especially for Gyeonggi residents, don't miss the

benefits and information provided by
each site.

Treasure Box of Outstanding Research Materials

·Policy Research Management System:
It is full of research service data conducted by the state on a budget, which includes the process of forming a game content-based technology platform (artificial intelligence, big data, blockchain, metaverse, Korean game and technology platform). We can read the results of a budget of more than tens of millions of won with one click. This information can

only be obtained by those who know it and those who have a habit of diligently searching. It also provides real estate-related policy data, such as the Suseong-gu Smart City Planning Service.

The information on local government sites is actually happening.

· Design contest for improvement of children's transportation park facilities in Gwangju Metropolitan City: Documents and postings on local government sites change and affect their lives. It's not a story in a novel, it's a real drive. Gwangju Metropolitan City promoted a contest to improve children's transportation park facilities for designers through the site, and as a result, selected the winning work and announced the winning work on the site. The city's general construction headquarters plans to sign a design contract in May and complete the design by September.

·Support for 'Earrow Store' in Incheon: Incheon Metropolitan City selects 10 small business owners who have maintained their traditions for more than 30 years without changing their businesses and supports environmental improvement, promotion, marketing, and production of promotional materials at 100% cost

I can suggest excellent examples of other local governments to the local governments where I live.

· Provision of home hospice relief medical services in Daejeon Metropolitan City: Information is provided to terminal patients and their families who want home hospice only in the country. It provides fluid therapy, management of various drainage pipes and bedsores, and family education and care for families if they wish to die at home. All you need is a doctor's note. Let's suggest that we want to receive such a service to the local government where I live due to online complaints. The judgment will be made by the local government, but the person in charge of other local governments does not know all of the services of other local governments. It can have a good influence.

Anyang Youth Wardrobe: It is a free rental service for interview suits. Jacket, pants, skirt, shoes, blouse, etc.

are rented free of charge up to five times a year per person for three nights and four days (Youth living in Anyang City (19-39 years old). If you sign up online, visit the site, and measure the size, you can receive it by courier. You can visit the rental company without having to go to Anyang City. For young people who cannot get a job, the cost of purchasing suits is also a burden. I hope other local governments will implement it.

Local government services

·Service by government 24: Employment, workplace, start-up, management, finance, tax, law, life, medical, death, marriage, childcare, education, environmental, disaster, soft power, crime, addiction, housing, real estate, public service, leisure, culture, and immigration.

·Service cases by field: 1,380 services are inquired when visiting detailed menu performances and cultural life menus in leisure, culture, and immigration countries. Among them, most of them are local services with 1,223. If you inquire in the latest order of the inquiry conditions, you will receive money information such as free opening events at the Jungnang-gu Sports Center swimming pool and payment of integrated cultural licenses for the underprivileged (there are many good information in other fields). Let's make a habit of searching for areas I need, such as information on truck rest areas (24 hours of free opening, available to general customers, and providing sleeping facilities, shower facilities, and laundry facilities). It's all a service run with my taxes. Even if I don't use it, let's share information with the neighbors around us.

If you look at the contents of the complaint, you can see the opportunity.

·Example of Haeundae-gu, Busan: Complaints are divided into open and closed information. Through the open counseling civil service inquiry menu, the current civil service counseling contents of local governments can be checked. These are specific and fact-based contents such as complaints that the floor of Haeundae's white sand is dangerous and unfriendliness of certain real estate. Residents living in the area can avoid dangerous roads, unfriendly store visits. In addition, it is possible to propose construction to the district office in the form of a promotion for businesses that play the role of local construction, etc. Another local government official can conduct activities to prevent complaints from local governments I manage in advance through complaints from other local governments. This is because complaints are unspecified individual activities, so they can appear over time without being expressed simultaneously.

·Problem-solving ability: Complaints are mostly problem-raising. It's a real problem, and it's a problem to be solved. Problem-solving skills are highly likely to be excellent for those who have gained experience in solving actual problems. If you want to develop problem-solving skills, think of yourself as the person in charge and try to find a solution. Let's also come up with the best strategy for the solution process. As well as public complaints, it helps you solve the problems you face in your life. Solving a lot of math problems, difficult quizzes, and improving IQ do not improve problem-solving skills. Even if the policy is implemented in consideration of the fact that it is happening in real life and that problems do not occur, the problem that inevitably occurred is civil complaints. It certainly helps to improve problem—solving skills.

Utilization of joint information of local governments, universities, hospitals, etc

·Gangwon Provincial University: It is the only university established and operated by Gangwon-do. In order to fulfill its role as a regional university, it provides regional economic revitalization through revitalization of industry-academic cooperation, opportunities for learning through backward studies programs and lifelong education, and information on employment and start-up support are provided as announcements. In the "Innovation Support Project" menu, operating information such as "Open Water Diver Course", "EFR First Aid Course", "3D Video Map Production Course", and "Online Store Operation Specialist Course" is provided (you can trust the curriculum in Gangwon-do).(15 million won for 14 start-up teams under the age of 39)

Chungcheongbuk-do National University: Public benefits in Korea are limited in the timing and quantity of applications. So information is money. Chungbuk Provincial University is a public university operated by Chungcheongbuk-do, so public benefits for young people are also posted on its website. For example, there is a project to support youth monthly rent in Okcheon-gun, Chungbuk (from 19 to 39 years old, to 180% or less of standard median disinfection, and up to 4 years of monthly rent of 100,000 won)

·Seoul Medical Center: It is a public hospital representing Seoul and develops and implements public medical services and public medical policies for Seoul citizens. It provides information on how to transfer public medical know-how at the national level. You can download the Seoul Medical Center Magazine called "Wangjin Bag" for free. Magazine is more detailed and accurate than medical books or information provided on portals, such as providing detailed information on Pax Robis, an eating treatment. In addition, there is information on the impact of long-term mask use on children's development, the days of the week, detailed hours of work, and specialized medical treatment at the

Seoul Medical Center, so it can be referred to when you want to receive medical treatment.

·Seoul Metropolitan Government Dental Hospital for the Disabled: Korea's welfare system is an application system even if it is mostly for recipients. This is because the manpower, resources, and budget are limited to benefit all targets. The notice to the dental hospital for the disabled is receiving applications for free dentures, prosthetics, and implants for the disabled. If you pay a little attention to the documents for those who have difficulty living around you and are suffering from tooth discomfort, you can present the joy of chewing, one of the five blessings.

Chapter 9 Utilizing Indirect Political Participation

a practical way to participate indirectly in politics

Participation in politics refers to a phenomenon in which sovereign citizens participate in the political process or participate in the policy-making process with an interest in the political phenomenon. So what is politics? Politics is about governing the country, that is, allowing people to lead human lives, coordinating mutual understanding, and correcting social order. All the state does to its people is politics.

Participation in politics is not just supporting lawmakers who agree or joining political parties. If you visit the Blue House website, anyone can read documents detailing the president's pledges, visions, and five-year action plans. The institutions that actually implement the pledge are ministries, local governments, and public institutions. The best way to make sure that the pledge is actually being made is to visit the agency's site. Attention may be paid to whether work is being carried out in accordance with the relevant government policy and whether the vision of the head of the agency is in the same direction as the government policy. In addition, you can present ideas related to it, or you can present your opinions as an open window to everyone, such as the sound of customers.

Those who say they should be interested in politics are only interested in related media reports and YouTube, and are busy spreading the contents to people around them. Of course, that would be one of the ways to be interested in politics. However, it is true political participation to visit the institution's site to pay attention and present opinions to see if the national policy is actually implemented as planned.

For example, before enacting or revising the law, the National

Assembly always announces the amendment for a certain period of time and collects opinions from any citizen. The revision of the law has a great impact on society as a whole. If the people are interested and express their opinions so that these laws are not revised in the wrong direction, the people can prevent the president or lawmakers from making the wrong choice. Don't just focus on news or SNS, visit the place where the actual politics is enforced, government-related sites, pay attention with hawk eyes, and participate.

If you look at the government 24 site, you can see the real power.

If you look at the organizational chart of any organization, you can see which department has power. It's simple: the direct department of the president or CEO is the strongest, and after that, the more likely it is to be an important organization. The Government 24 site has a government/local organization chart. Everyone may be curious about the government organization chart once they watch the news or stop by a government office. This government organization chart also has a site called Government 24. Once again, the information released on the site is the most accurate and up-to-date.

According to the government's organizational chart, the presidential direct department consists of the presidential secretary's office, the National Security Office, the presidential security office, the National Rights Commission, and the crime investigation office for high-ranking public officials. The

Ministry of Strategy and Finance, the Financial Services Commission, the People's Rights Commission, the Nuclear Safety Commission, the Ministry of Agriculture, Food and Drug Safety, the Ministry of Strategy and Finance, the Ministry of Science, ICT, the Ministry of Foreign Affairs, the Ministry, the Ministry of Health, the Ministry, the Ministry of Health, the Ministry, the Ministry, the Ministry. In addition, public institutions, etc. belong to the subordinate institutions of each department listed above.

At least, if you know what the Korean information organization chart looks like, wherever you go and listen to any news, it will be organically drawn, which will help you understand and judge the situation.

Site examples of the Ministry of Public Administration and Security

If you go to the site of the Ministry of Public Administration and Security, you can get administrative safety statistics and various visualization data. No matter what topic you present, there will be more than one relevant piece of data, and you will gain trust by identifying the data source with the Ministry of the Interior and Safety and citing statistics and visual data. In addition, it will give the impression that you are a talented person who can use information widely, such as the Ministry of the Interior and Safety.

If you look at the Government Innovation Coordination Office among the organizational menus of the Ministry of the Interior and Safety, you can check the Ministry of the Interior and Safety's business promotion plan for 21 years. It can be referred to in presenting trends in bidding for government-related institutions in business preparation, and if it is used as explanatory data in ppt, it presents government policies that the ordering party did not know and has an image of a very advanced businessman.

In addition, there is the Ministry of the Interior and Safety's Local Human Resources Development Institute, and if you look at the article recruiting an active administration monitoring team, a letter of appointment is issued and a prize money is also provided. There is a lot of good information for those who want to review their work, prepare for college entrance, or gain various experiences through surveys, SNS promotions.

In addition, you can challenge yourself to apply for an innovation project to regulate people's livelihoods, have the opportunity to present a ministerial award (with prizes), and use one more line on your profile to prepare for college entrance and employment. The documents of the Ministry of the Interior and Safety are a standard form of documents for public officials and public enterprises, and there are many documents to refer to if you want to make decent documents.

Now, this is why I can't help but study the site. Let's visit the site and get real information. It is not gossip that you read once and forget, but

real information that is directly
connected to life.

Chapter 10 From hobbies to volunteer work

Useful sites for blogging

·Reviews: You can see the current level of my blog. You can check your blog quality index and search ranking, and there is a Naver login process.

·Blog Chart: Weekly and theme charts for each field can be viewed by date. When blogs grow to a certain extent, they give you fun to look up. It also provides my blog analysis function. It motivates me to continue to develop in the process of checking the level of my blog.

·SuperMembers: When the operator who runs the Naver blog enters the Naver ID, the blog ranking can be checked and the estimated advertising cost can be inquired once.

·Black Kiwi: It is a big data-based keyword analysis platform. When searching for a keyword called diet, it shows the search volume by keyword rating, monthly PC, and mobile, and also shows related keywords. If so, use keywords with high expected search volume on your blog. Exposure

and search are better, so my blog will
be searched more.

I'm going to do volunteer work intelligently

The Seoul Volunteer Center site recruits a happy empathy volunteer group every year. You can receive a letter of appreciation if you participate in briquette volunteer work more than twice with the lottery fund. You can check if the lottery you live in really contributes to society, and add a line of self-introduction such as your child's college admissions as an auditor. Let's have a volunteer history with a theme, not a boring volunteer work performance. If you are a social worker, community service activities with various themes for each local government become a good experience. At this time, if you want to help a neighbor in need purely with cash, you can share it directly with the neighbor you met through volunteer work. I recommend it to someone who is anxious to leave a bundle of money to a charity (not distrust the charity, but doubt it depending on the person). This kind of person (me too) In the same case, they do not donate at all, so I think it is meaningful if they can practice sharing even to their confirmed neighbors.)

Useful Sites for Moving Out

·Reservation system for discharging waste home appliances: You can make a reservation for free visit collection when handling waste home appliances that are not used when moving.

·Changing mail address collectively: Civil petition 24, government 24, and community service centers can also apply.

·Cowon Energy Service: Urban gas transfer reporting service allows you to easily apply for urban gas connection and demolition at once. You can access the information by searching the portal for urban gas transfer. Still, it is different from approaching knowing that there is a site like this.

·Florplanner: You can simulate the arrangement of furniture. 2D, 3D floor plan functionality

a free music composition site

·Band Lab: You can download your

own musical notes in various sound quality. You can also sell your own music or album. You can make an album by weaving music, and do it for free. Various compositional instruments are provided, and their own guitar and piano are connected to provide a recording function with the device.

Identify trends

If you want to know the trend of products such as mobile phones, cars, and refrigerators, visit representative sites such as 00 Electronics and 00 cars, and promote new models that have not yet begun to be sold better than any other media. Other media often post promotional posts on this site. Rather than seeing someone's post belatedly, if you search for related information directly on the site, you become an insider. For example, if you go to Hyundai Motor's website, you can see Hyundai Motor by regiment from 1960 to 2020. Anyone who designs cars can check the trend of car design. Rather than searching for the second and third rounds of information that someone has organized and delivered belatedly, they first encounter the information on the institution's site, which will be released first.

Information and Communication Entry Course

The Information and Communication Terminology Dictionary, a site of the Korea Information and Communication Technology Association, is a site that searches for IT terms and displays the results. It is not just a lexicon in a word dictionary way, but when you search for a word, it shows the relationship diagram of the terms related to the word, just below the description of the word. This relationship map moves like it's alive, and when you click on a secondary word of interest, the term relationship map related to the word unfolds.

Disclosure information of obligations of public institutions

In accordance with the Public Institution's Information Disclosure Act, public institutions are required to actively disclose information held and managed by public institutions as prescribed by this Act to guarantee the public's right to know.

If you're exploring public institution sites or if you're exploring them more deeply, you can get additional information under this law.

The relevant site is an information disclosure site. Most of the information, which is not confidential, is open to the public or partially disclosed. Even if it is a partial disclosure, some information can be disclosed.

· Information disclosure portal: All public institutions and local governments in Korea can inquire information disclosed among official documents generated by thousands of cases every day. It is configured to conveniently search for information by subject.It also provides (health, economy, education, regulatory reform, welfare, safety, leisure, childcare, jobs, housing, administrative finance, environment), and best information collection functions.

Patent information search

Patent Information Net (Kipris) is a public patent information search service operated by the Korea Patent Information Service so that users can search and view all information related to domestic and foreign intellectual property rights held by the Korean Intellectual Property Office through the Internet.

It provides information on domestic intellectual property rights such as patents, utility models, designs, trademarks, and referees, and overseas patents in 12 countries, including the United States, Europe, and Japan. It also provides various additional functions in addition to search functions.(My Interested Patent Service, Visiting Patent Service, Patent Search Toolbar, My Folder, Popular Search Terms, etc.)

· U.S. Patent and Trademark Office, Europe, Japan, Denmark, Mexico,

Switzerland, Slovakia, UK, Australia, Finland, Germany, Luxembourg, France, Spain, Austria, China, Taiwan, Sweden, Hungary, Hong Kong, Canada (most overseas patent and patent office sites are available in English, making it convenient to use)

Chapter 11 Use for Travel

Travel Plan Information Site

It's a waste to make up your mind and go on a trip with your family or important people. If you want to stay in a good place and have a healing trip for a limited time as much as possible, it is better to check and plan information in advance. The site aimed only at providing this information is Korea Tourism Organization.

It is also a way to travel after searching on portals or SNS, but in some cases, due to biased information, it is not good in reality, or it is too known that people only visit. Let's use a site that provides all tourism information evenly without information.

· Korea Tourism Organization: It provides all information on domestic travel, including restaurants in every corner of Korea, accommodation information, and local events. If you don't want to plan a trip, use the travel planner function. Information such as course trips made by professional planners is abundant. Guidebooks that can only be obtained locally, can be downloaded in advance from this site.

· Ministry of Culture, Sports and Tourism: There is a lot of specific information about domestic culture and local festivals. It is also full of performance information and art-related information. Information on local festivals, recommended destinations, cultural and artistic performances, and sports events can be inquired by region at the Menu Culture Square, and a list of cultural and artistic performances can be downloaded at once, so you can choose from the whole without inquiring. If you travel alone, watching art performances is better when you do it alone, so let's refer to it.

· Ministry of Foreign Affairs Overseas Safety Travel: Before traveling abroad, you can check the safety of the country now. Despite warning that it is dangerous, there may be restrictions on help in the country if you visit overseas forcibly. When downloading an overseas safety travel app, text an acquaintance with location information through an emergency contact registered in case of an emergency

It can be transmitted immediately, and real-time push notifications for travel alerts by country can be provided. Let's also save the consular call center number. It provides 24-hour 24/7 interpretation services in seven languages, including English and Chinese, in case of an incident, accident, or emergency.

· International Work Camp Organization: You can experience various things such as travel, volunteer work, and cultural experience at a low cost of participation. Let's visit the site from time to time like visiting a friend's house. The work camp is an international exchange program where young people from different cultures gather for one to three weeks to do volunteer work and cultural exchanges, which costs about 2.2 million won in Europe and 1.35 million won in Asia. It's much cheaper than personal travel expenses, and there's a lot to gain from a 100-year-old program. In addition, due to language training, there are cases where you go abroad with more than 10 million won in expenses, and you can go to around 2 million won through overseas volunteer work camps. Activities can be selected from 1 to 4 weeks, and many participants choose 2-week activities the most considering the travel schedule before and after. Only participants who participate in the activity for more than two weeks can choose two or more regions and can also be with friends (up to three people). During the participation period, it is arranged on several projects on a weekly basis, allowing various experiences and exchanges with various volunteers. In New Zealand, it mainly focuses on local national parks, environmental protection zones, and beaches.

  - Example of a day's schedule for overseas volunteer activities: wake-up-breakfast-take a briefing on volunteer activities-take a briefing on volunteer activities-take a necessary skill, safety rules-take a volunteer start-coffee break-lunch hours-take a break-take a break-home-getting-out dinner and eat-free time

European Travel Readiness Site

·Incheon Airport: In addition to the flight operation inquiry, the check-in counter and each gate are displayed when changing. When traveling with family, lovers, or company employees, you can become an insider without wandering at the airport. Delayed flights are also displayed, and SMS can also be used to receive notification messages about delays and cancellations.

·European Festival, Holiday Inquiry: If you check the festival schedule in Spain, England, Switzerland, and

France in advance, you can enjoy a special trip to Europe. It also provides travel plans, transportation, currency exchange, exchange rates, mobile phones, lodging and lodging tips, and even tips on not lining up for tourism and experience.

·C-ticket: It is a reservation site for various overseas musicals, concerts, and exhibitions. The major reservation countries are Canada, Denmark, Spain, France and the Netherlands. Portugal, Switzerland. It is the United Kingdom, the United States, and so on.

·CityMapper: It is a site as good as

Google Map when traveling abroad, and cityMapper is convenient when taking a bus in London. The location of the bus I got on may come out, and the place I get off may not be too far. It is more convenient to use it as an app. It is serving 71 European cities in 31 countries. With the CityMapper PASS card, a single transportation card is available for most transportation in Europe.

Chapter 12 Extension of Site Utilization

Cross-utilization of information

If you are a proposer, you can suggest the idea of Institute A to Institute B. In addition, even if you are looking to apply for Institute A's idea contest, you can also cross-use information from other similar or completely different institution sites.

Although the information is equal, the quality and nature of the business are operated much differently than expected depending on the activities and will of the executives and employees of the institution.

Even if the same law is revised, it is only feared that the law has been revised, but it does not visit each and every one of them and explain it to the institution. The institution that has found out that the law has been revised will quickly prepare and apply it so that the business is not damaged, and the institution that ignores the information will apply the amendment only after it is pointed out by the audit agency.

As such, the degree of information retention or use by each institution is not more equal than you think. This is why it is necessary to visit institutional sites to explore and compare information, and to have a sense of where and what information is.

The input and output of a search

The process of obtaining results from search activities is divided into information input and output. The material of the input of information refers to all the media in the world. Typical input materials are books, videos such as YouTube, and institutional sites. Here, we are talking about the benefits of the institutional site, so we are talking about the institutional site input.

First, list the materials obtained by searching or searching for information on the agency site. The information listed is now grouped among similar personalities. And draw a relationship map of the groups using a mind map method. The results so far alone make the only list of information meaningful and bring up ideas. Furthermore, segmentation searches are performed on information that is considered interesting and important among the listed materials in the group. This is because all information is different in size, and some information contains more information.

It now adds a summary sentence that

can be expressed in a single line in a group of information. Now look at the new information structures that you've created, and if you have the order or direction of the information, you can define a new process. In addition, new models or templates can be created. You just understood the steps to analyze and utilize the results of searching for information.

Korea's Data Warehouse

Recently, the Korean government aims to become a data economy powerhouse by strengthening the opening and use of public data. In this regard, the Ministry of Public Administration and Security operates a public data portal.

The data classification system allows selective inquiry into public administration, science and technology, education, transportation logistics, land management, agriculture, fisheries, culture and tourism, law, health care, social welfare, industrial employment, food health, disaster safety, financial finance, and unification and foreign security.

The site discloses free data accumulated in information systems built and developed by government agencies such as public institutions with huge budgets.

Rather, individuals can create meaningful new information by combining data from each institution disclosed here.

Creating a Site

· You look at things that exist and you ask why, but I dream of things that don't exist and ask why not. – The George Bernard Shaw –

How much benchmarking and case studies are conducted between companies and public institutions? Since it is difficult to perform its original work, there are visits to other institutions or sites to solve problems directly, but active visits to sites of other institutions are rare.

What does this say? I can organize a site menu consisting of the best harmonized information by searching and comparing information on the representative or detailed sites of the agency between similar groups or completely heterogeneous groups.

Let's say you're running a small business, so you have to create a business site. Even if it is left to the website producer, the ordering person can be involved in the composition of the site's menu to some extent. At this time, you visit similar or other business sites to benchmark only the menu composition that suits your taste. Of course, due to your usual interest in business, if you were exploring similar sites, the benchmarking period would be reduced.

If you searched for information on other institutions' sites and combined the new site menu composition, a site that was not in the world was born.

Isn't imitation the mother of creation? It's easier than you think to dream and achieve what didn't exist.

Overseas site

<<You can get the effect of overseas business trips by visiting overseas sites.>>

When the site search technology of Korean institutions and companies increases to some extent, let's look at similar overseas sites. Because people live in the same place, similar sites can be found on overseas sites.

Using tools such as Naver Papago, it

is convenient to use a service that always translates and displays the English of a web page into Korean. If the overseas site URL does not appear as a primary search, it may be necessary to visit through a related encyclopedia or a secondary site. In addition, if you visit one overseas site, you often provide link information of related agencies within the site, so you can expand the scope of overseas site discovery by biting your tail.

◇ Visit domestic sites → Visit similar sites overseas → Expand through links within overseas sites

· Tesla: This is an overseas Tesla site run by Elon Musk. It is highly likely that the latest models and trends will be checked before Korean magazines and news.

· United States Census: It is the official U.S. government statistics site. It is an open site that provides various high-quality data, including U.S. demographics, for free without subscription. It is provided by a method such as a data search function, microdata, and a user-defined table, not simply data in an Excel list.

· UK Tourism Board: Provides up-to-date UK tourism information. It provides information for travelers, useful links, British traditions, sports, shopping, royal family, food, and art culture.

Since it is operated by the government like the information of Korea's Tourism Organization, reliable and up-to-date information can be checked.

· CIA: You can also visit the CIA's official site, which you've only heard of in movies. The CIA's vision, mission, organization, and recruitment information are disclosed. The recruitment field is diverse, including analysis methodologists, targeting analysts, economic analysts, and military analysts, and even annual salaries will be disclosed. For example, it is disclosed that targeting analysts use data sets, specialized tools, and network analysis techniques to identify and analyze threats to the United States and identify opportunities to disrupt them, with starting salaries ranging from $59,824 to $176,300 (W75 million to 230 million).

◇ It's fun to make a list of domestic sites that you're interested in and break the seal of each overseas site!

In order to strengthen the competitiveness of a country or individual, it is not necessary to visit the country to obtain information. The priority is to check information on government sites run by each country, and you will probably be able to make full use of most of the information you want.

In addition, you need to know some English, so you can enter the desired search term and infer the desired site name.

If you can speak foreign languages other than English, you can use the site information of a wider country. If you can speak more foreign languages, you can experience a wider world. This is one of the reasons why I study foreign languages.

◇ Using overseas sites with web English translator → I want to study various foreign languages because I am curious about more sites in more countries! (Killing two birds with one stone, developing foreign language skills, and acquiring more information on overseas sites!)

epilogue

If you follow this book and use it on the site, you will know how much information is overflowing in the world.

The key is how many people and various purposes the disclosed information is being used.

Information is only valuable when it is utilized. The government's vision is to become a data powerhouse and put energy into data disclosure and integration because information is power and money.

The utility of the site covered here is only the tip of the iceberg. It is sufficient to achieve the purpose of putting your foot in the door of the site's use. to visit one or two sitesIf you look at it, it will open up a new world of site information.

Hopefully, readers of this book will utilize a lot of high-quality information generated on the site, and the effect of using site information in each field will be exerted to achieve individual goals and help national competitiveness.